PECK
HIGH SCHOOL

Golden Years Remembered

WHAT OTHERS ARE SAYING

"The full story of the William Henderson Peck High School has been untold since its founding as Colored School No. 1 to its rich legacy and tradition of nurturance and education. In Annette Myers, we have a celebrated writer and Peckite who knows the history and tells the story of a people, place, and time in the historic city of Fernandina on Amelia Island, Florida. Like so many other stories of African- American experiences and achievements, this story is America's story."

—E. Veronica Pace, great-granddaughter of William Henderson Peck

"I applaud Mrs. Myers for taking the time to put together this important history noting the early years of Peck High School and other historical events that took place during those times. This is the first published book chronicling the history of Peck High School established years ago to educate colored citizens in the Fernandina Community."

—Narvea Clem Gardner, son of Florida Robinson Gardner and great-grandnephew of Father Lewis Cook

"Mrs. Myers gives a documented account of the early years of Peck High School plus bits of early Fernandina history, United States history, and the making of African-American history paralleling the golden years of Peck High School. This book is of interest to anyone interested in the history of Peck High School and for generations to come."

—Rev. Jeremiah Robinson, Jr., pastor of New Zion Missionary Church

"It is important that we document the history of Peck High School before all of our history is lost in time. Thanks to Annette Myers for sharing her knowledge of our history and other bits of local and African-American history."

—Neil Frink, Peck High School class of 1959,
president of Peck Alumni Association, A.L. Lewis Historical Society,
and African-American History of Amelia Island

"This book by Annette Myers is an invaluable part of the history of Peck High School including other historical information she has referenced."

—Charles L. Albert, Jr., Peck High School class of 1949,
president of NCCDC, Peck High School science teacher and former
mayor of Fernandina Beach

P E C K
High School

Golden Years Remembered

Annette McCollough Myers

PECK HIGH SCHOOL: GOLDEN YEARS REMEMBERED

Library of Congress Control Number: 2017936874

FIRST EDITION (Hardcover) ISBN 978-0-9966687-4-3

Published by Giro di Mondo Publishing,
a subsidiary of the Ottima Group, LLC
Fernandina Beach, FL

Contact info@girodimondo.com

Printed in the United States of America

Edited by Emily W. Carmain

10 9 8 7 6 5 4 3 2 1

This book is dedicated to my father,
Wendell Herbert (W.H.) McCollough,
who was the godson of
Professor William Henderson (W.H.) Peck.
Wendell H. was initialed after Professor W.H. Peck.
W.H. McCollough graduated from Peck High School in 1936.
He passed away on March 19, 1993
in Fernandina Beach, Florida.

Secondly, this book is dedicated
to all who have passed on
and all who still cherish
the fond memories of Peck High School.

CONTENTS

THE EARLY YEARS OF FERNANDINA, FLORIDA

Center Street Fernandina Fla.

PREFACE

$\mathcal{T}$he period from 1885 to 1969 marked eighty-four years in the existence of a school establishment in Fernandina, Nassau County, Florida, for the education of African-American children.

From 1911 to 1969 marked fifty-eight years that African-American students of the community had the opportunity to graduate from Peck High School, named for Professor William Henderson Peck.

The purpose of this book is to further document and bring some of the scattered early pieces of history together regarding Peck High School, including bits and pieces of African-American history and other historical events during the early years of Peck.

11

Since 1983, there have been five grand reunions held to bring former students, teachers, administrators and staff, family, friends and the community together. The first and second grand reunions were held under the leadership of Elmo V. Myers, who was president and founder of the Nassau County Community Development Corporation called NCCDC. Mr. Myers was a 1948 graduate of Camden County Training School in Woodbine, Georgia, and the husband of Annette McCollough Myers.

The idea of the first reunion of classes was adopted by the Myerses from the grand reunion held by former students of Ralph Bunch High School, formerly known as Camden County Training School.

Every effort was made by officers and members of NCCDC

and the community to sponsor the 1983 and 1985 grand reunions of Peck chaired by Mr. Myers' wife, Annette, who was a 1955 graduate of Peck High School.

This movement also sparked the idea of bringing about and putting together the initial history of Peck High School, undertaken by Willie Mae Ashley, which was entered in the first grand reunion booklet of 1983.

Today in 2017, after one hundred and thirty-two years, the legacy of the first African-American school in Fernandina, Florida, the legacy of Professor Peck and the legacy of Peck High School continue to live on.

ACKNOWLEDGEMENTS

*A*cknowledgements for this publication go to Mrs. Florida Cook Robinson Gardner. Several years ago, Mrs. Gardner sent to me old Peck School graduation programs and other information that she wanted me to have. I am grateful to this loving lady for allowing me to become the caretaker of her historical documents. Those documents also had belonged to her aunt, Mrs. Alleen Cook Bradley. Mrs. Bradley was a 1916 Peck High School graduate, a great community historian, public speaker, Peck school teacher, and the wife of Reverend Gus Clemon (G.C.) Bradley.

Not knowing what I would do with this important information, beginning in 1891 with Colored School No. 1, I held on to Mrs. Gardner's records up to this writing in 2016.

Mrs. Robinson Gardner was a 1941 Peck High School graduate. She passed away in Vero Beach, Florida, on November 29, 2014, at the age of ninety-two. Having spent much of her adult life in Cocoa, Florida, she was buried in Cocoa.

Acknowledgements also go to the representatives of the various graduating classes who were kind enough to give the NCCDC initial grand reunion committee of 1983 a list of their graduating classes and other information they wanted to share.

An abundance of thanks goes to my noteworthy and patient editor guru, Emily Carmain. I am grateful to my longtime friend and publisher, Raffaela Marie Rizzo Fenn, and her husband, Mark Fenn, of Giro di Mondo Publishing for their enthusiasm and time-consuming efforts in this project.

My great appreciation and many thanks also go to my other very special colleagues, family and friends who shared in this memorable keepsake book.

"Remembering our history
and turning back the hands of time."

~ Annette Myers

WILLIAM HENDERSON PECK
1859-1950
Buried in Bosque Bello Cemetery

In 2000, Professor Peck was nominated for the distinguished Great Floridian Award. He was noted as principal of the Nassau Colored School No. 1, for expanding the curriculum to a full high school, and for the many years he served.

HISTORY OF PECK HIGH SCHOOL

*P*eck High School had its beginning when a petition was circulated and a resolution was offered by Henry Beard Delaney (1858-1928) for the erection of a high school building for the training of the race (colored) in Fernandina. (Taken from a newspaper article in the *Florida Mirror*, January 1, 1880.)

The action to establish a school for African-Americans in Fernandina marked a significant advancement, by the colored community, as prior to that, African-American students had not attended school the same number of days as white students. A school was built in 1884 and opened to students in 1885.

17

Professor Moses H. Payne of Washington, D.C., came to Fernandina to teach in a four-room, two-story building at the 11th Street site near Centre Street that was opened in 1885. He was also the school's first principal.

Professor William Henderson (W.H.) Peck, also of Washington, D.C., and reportedly a graduate of Howard University, came to Fernandina in 1887 as an assistant to Professor Payne. As the school grew, two more rooms were added in 1892 and six teachers were employed.

Professor Payne died during the yellow fever epidemic of 1888 and Professor Peck was appointed principal. In 1892, the new Colored School No. 1 soon became District School No. 2.

In 1910-1911, the Board of Education decided to name one of the county schools, white or colored, for the principal having served the longest.

Since Professor Peck had served longer, he was given the privilege of having the school named for him. Hence, District School No. 2 was given the name Peck High. Professor Peck served for almost fifty years.

The first graduating class was in 1891. This class contained six graduates. By 1894, the school had all grades up to tenth grade until 1908, when it expanded to include grades one through twelve. The first senior high class graduated in 1908.

The present Peck building, located in the 500 block of South 11th Street, was erected in 1927, but was not occupied until January 1928.

There was a rapid increase in enrollment and a bond issue was floated in 1949, giving an addition of four rooms to Peck High. This primary building was erected at the same site and annexed to Peck on the 10th Street side in 1950.

In 1956, a gymnasium was constructed and a new building, including a cafeteria, was built for elementary students. The building for elementary students, demolished in June 1990, was located south of and across from the Peck building.

In 1968-69, Peck students were integrated with other schools and the site became a third-grade center. The last graduating class was the class of 1968-69. Over time, the Peck building became totally abandoned, deteriorated, and was used as a storage facility.

Principals who served from Professor Peck's time included William V. Nixon, T. Tillinghast, W.H. Bullock, Edyth J, Thurston, William Green, A. Quinn Jones, Jr., James B. Bryant,

Roscoe Webb, W.D. Hicks, Maurice Barnett, R.T. Anderson; and Rutha Bell Person Morgan, office secretary and interim administrator.

Peck has played an important part in our nation, at home and abroad, in the education of many African-American citizens. Trained under the laws of segregation, limited resources, insufficient books or no textbooks, inadequate building and heating facilities, Peck's students, past and present—who attended between 1891 and 1969—are among the most prominent American citizens. Peck has produced an array of outstanding doctors, lawyers, musicians, ministers, morticians, authors, government officials, educators, business administrators, military officials, manufacturers, CEOs, and numerous trade and technical professionals.

———◄•►———

NOTES

Today, the Peck Center, renamed by the city, serves as an important community facility and is used by city officials and non-profit organizations, for classes, community activities, and recreation.

A state historic marker was placed at the school site on Friday, February 19, 2016, by the Peck Alumni Association.

The William H. Peck Memorial Scholarship is awarded annually to an eligible high school senior in Nassau County by the Nassau County Community Development Corporation.

Henry Beard Delany, who became an Episcopal Bishop in 1918, was the father of the famous Delany sisters, Sadie and Bessie Delany.

In 2010, the Peck Center was included in the city's historic district. The building serves as a significant component of the story of African-American history and heritage in Fernandina Beach and Nassau County.

Some of the above facts were obtained from a 1959-60 Peck High School student handbook, 1983 and 1985 grand reunion booklets, the internet, other reunion booklets, news clippings and lectures.

In this edition, you will note variations in the spelling of the Delany family surname, such as Delaney and DeLaney, as the name was recorded at the time.

WHERE GRADUATIONS WERE HELD BEGINNING 1907 UNTIL THE PECK GYMNASIUM WAS BUILT IN 1956

New Zion (Missionary) Baptist Church

Top photo, as it was built in 1907. Bottom photo, as it stands today. The Fellowship Hall, at left of the church, was built in 1977 under church trustee and local contractor Elliott "Tex" McGowen.

Peck gymnasium—built in 1956

PECK HIGH SCHOOL
FERNANDINA BEACH, FLA.

23

ELEMENTARY SCHOOL
FERNANDINA BEACH, FLA.

Peck buildings as they looked in 1956

City of Fernandina Beach Peck Center sign

Roll Call of Classes
&
Historical Events

1891-1931

"Education is the key
to unlock the golden door of freedom."

~ George Washington Carver

CLASS OF 1891

NETTIE ANDERSON OWENS
EMMA PRICE BAILEY
J. CAREPTA LANG
SARA E. DELANEY NOBLES
ELIZABETH ROBERTS
CHARLES (SUMMER) ROBINSON

1891 — Consisting of six students named above, these were the first graduates of the new Colored School No. 1. President Benjamin Harrison, the 23rd president of the United States, was in office at the time.

The Nassau County Courthouse, located at 416 Centre Street, in Fernandina Beach was constructed in 1891.

Built in 1891 was Trinity United Methodist Church (below), located at the corner of Ash and 8th streets. Trinity was also the home church of Professor Peck.

Class of 1892

Minnie Butler
Cora Perry Evans
Joseph McCleary
Charlie McCleary
Dr. Jake Hughes

1892 — The new Colored School No. 1 became District School Number 2.

Sarah Boone, African-American inventor,
patented and improved the ironing board in 1892
for ironing sleeves and intricate parts of ladies' clothing.

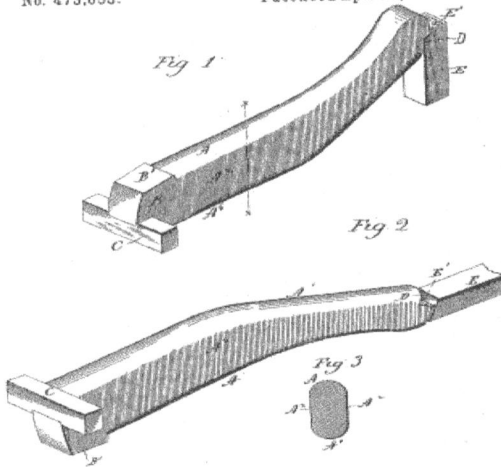

CLASS OF 1893

ROSA B. LANG HOOPER
ALMA PETERSON
HATTIE WILLIAMS
MARY E. HARRIS STAYS
ALEX VERDIER
JOHN BONARD
SALLIE CRUMP
SARAH SPAULDING

The year that this class graduated, inventor Thomas Alva Edison introduced the age of the electric lighting system and completed the building of the first motion picture camera in New Jersey, in 1893.

Daniel Hale Williams, an African-American doctor, performed the first successful open heart surgery in 1893. Dr. Williams also founded an interracial and first black-owned hospital in the United States (Provident Hospital, Chicago).

29

American General Surgeon — Daniel Hale Williams
January 18, 1856 – August 4, 1931

1894

No Class Recorded

Coca-Cola was first marketed and sold in bottles.

The automatic time clock system, still used in schools today, was invented and patented.

30

SIXTH STREET—Fernandina.

6th Street in Fernandina in 1894

CLASS OF 1895

DR. M. F. McCLEARY
EDWARD ROBERTS
J. H. STAYS, JR.
MARY PERRY PUGH
SOLARIES WILLIAMS
FLORENCE COOK BURNETTE
JANIE HAWKINS TAYLOR

In 1895, an improved moving picture projector was patented.

The 1891 Buckeye gas-driven patented auto was known to be the first for-sale auto in the U.S.

Buckeye gasoline buggy

CLASS OF 1898

MOLLIE BUTLER LIGGINS
WINNIE FRED PERRY
LILLIE O. HARRIS

The North Carolina Mutual Life Insurance Company, founded in 1898 as the North Carolina Mutual and Provident Association, is the largest black-owned insurance company in the world today.

This year began the use of postcards by the United States Postal Service.

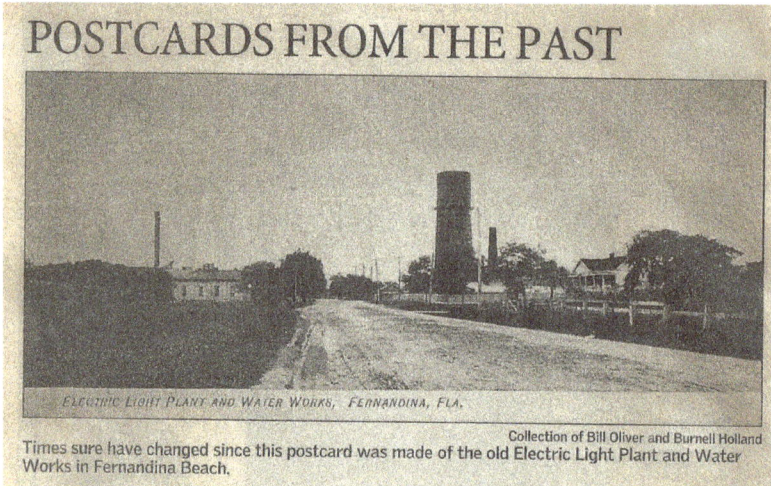

POSTCARDS FROM THE PAST

ELECTRIC LIGHT PLANT AND WATER WORKS, FERNANDINA, FLA.

Collection of Bill Oliver and Burnell Holland
Times sure have changed since this postcard was made of the old Electric Light Plant and Water Works in Fernandina Beach.

New Zion Baptist Church, as it appeared from 1878 to 1907, can be seen at far left.

CLASS OF 1899

JOE ARGRETT
ROSA TRAEYE

This year began the use of voting machines by Congress for federal elections.

The train depot, 102 Centre Street, in Fernandina Beach was opened for business in 1899.

**Train depot,
now the Welcome Center of Fernandina Beach**

33

CLASS OF 1900

IDA SYE PINKNEY

James Weldon Johnson penned the song "Lift Every Voice and Sing." His brother, J. Rosamond Johnson, put the lyrics to music.

Rosamond Johnson (left) and James Weldon Johnson

1901

No Class Recorded

Florida's first Afro-American Insurance Company was founded May 3, 1901, in Jacksonville, Florida, under the leadership of Abraham Lincoln (A.L.) Lewis.

Home Office: Afro-American Life Insurance Co., Jacksonville, Fla.

Jacksonville, Florida

Home office, Afro-American Life Insurance Company, as it appeared in early years

35

CLASS OF 1902

ANNIE HAZEL JOHNSON
EDWARD DAY

Modern air conditioning was first heard of, invented, and used around 1902.

36

Ships and trains at lumber dock — Fernandina, 1902

CLASS OF 1903

ANNIE ROBINSON WILSON
ADOLPHUS LEWIS

Around 1903, abolitionist and humanitarian Harriett Tubman (born in 1820) gave her home, in Auburn, New York, to the African Methodist Episcopal Zion Church for the elderly. She was admitted to live in her own donated home from 1911 until her death in 1913.

Harriett Tubman late in life

37

CLASS OF 1904

THERESA ROBINSON
ANNIE KENT
CASSIE PERRY

This was the year that attorney James C. Napier, of Nashville, Tennessee, founded the first black-owned bank, the One Cent Savings Bank for African-Americans (now called Citizens Bank).

Mary McLeod Bethune founded Bethune-Cookman College in Daytona Beach, Florida.

Mary McLeod Bethune with girls from the school

CLASS OF 1905

ELIZABETH TRAEYE
BERTHA JONES
EUNICE BRAWLEY

Sarah Breedlove Walker, a self-made millionaire, known as Madam C.J. Walker, founded her own hair care and cosmetics business and the method for straightening and softening African-American hair.

An authentic antique Seth Thomas "King Bee" wall clock, circa 1905, below, by the L.B. Price Company of Kansas City, Missouri, that belonged to the author's grandmother.

CLASS OF 1906

IDA BRUTON COOK
BEATRICE WILLIS ALBERT

Paul Laurence Dunbar, poet and publisher, was born in 1872 and died February 9, 1906.

We Wear the Mask

Paul Laurence Dunbar, 1872-1906

We wear the mask that grins and lies,
It hides our cheeks and shades our eyes, —
This debt we pay to human guile;
With torn and bleeding hearts we smile
And mouth with myriad subtleties,

Why should the world be over-wise,
In counting all our tears and sighs?
Nay, let them only see us, while
We wear the mask.

We smile, but oh great Christ, our cries
To thee from tortured souls arise.
We sing, but oh the clay is vile
Beneath our feet, and long the mile,
But let the world dream otherwise,
We wear the mask!

CLASS OF 1907

MARY JOHNSON DICKERSON
ROBERT JOHNSON

New Zion Baptist Church, 10 South 10th Street, was destroyed by fire in 1907 and was rebuilt in the same year.

New Zion — original church built in 1878 under Father Lewis Cook — is the wooden edifice, second building from the left, with bell tower.

CLASS OF 1908

JAMES DIXON
CHARLIE ROBERT

For the first time, the Colored school that later became the Peck School consisted of grades one through twelve.

**A typical classroom setting, above, in the early 1900s
and beyond, in places where African-Americans were
privileged to attend school.**

CLASS OF 1909

EMMETT KELLY
HARRY TRAEYE
RUBY SMITH

The National Association for the Advancement of Colored People (NAACP) was founded in New York City.

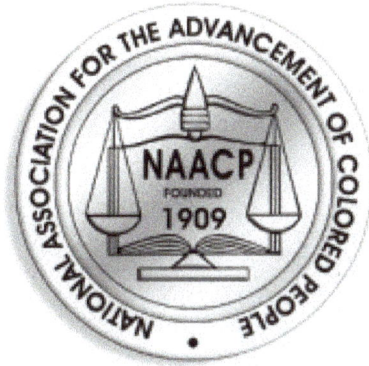

NAACP Emblem

CLASS OF 1910

PRENELLA HARRIS CRIBB
ERMA ARCHER
ERNESTINE LANGLEY

Jack Johnson was the first black boxer to win the world heavyweight boxing title, in his first controversial interracial boxing match for what was called the "Fight of the Century." Including this match and other matches, he held the heavyweight title from 1908 to 1915.

The *Crisis* became the official magazine of the NAACP.

THE

SOULS OF BLACK FOLK

ESSAYS AND SKETCHES

BY

W. E. BURGHARDT DU BOIS

SECOND EDITION

CHICAGO
A. C. McCLURG & CO.
1903

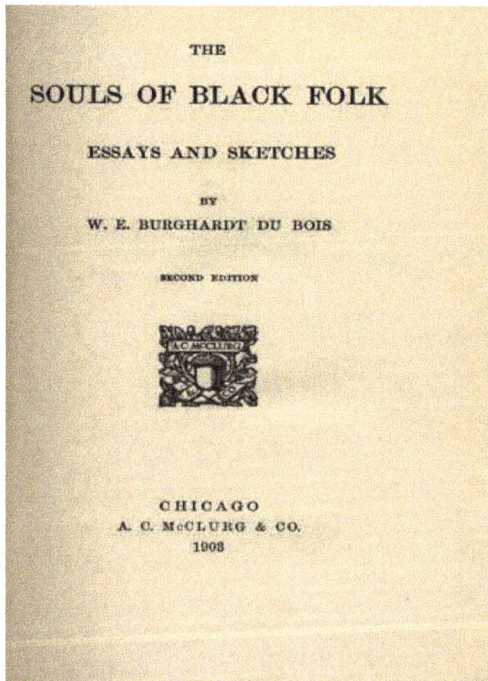

Crisis magazine by W.E.B. DuBois

CLASS OF 1911

LOUISE CRIBB REFOE
ERNEST STAYS
PRENELLA ROBERTS
GRACE ARCHER
GLADYS REYNOLDS

District School No. 2 was named the Peck School.

The same year, Charles W. Chappelle, African-American aviation pioneer and medal winner, successfully invented, designed and displayed his long-distance airplane in New York City.

GLENDA S. JENKINS/NEWS-LEADER
E. Veronica Pace stands with a portrait of her great-grandfather, Professor William Henderson Peck, principal of Peck High School starting in 1887.

Great-granddaughter of Professor Peck

CLASS OF 1912

CARRIE LOU GILBERT
GAINES REED
ANNIE REYNOLDS
LILLIE REED STAYS

African-American composer W.C. Handy self-published "The Memphis Blues."

A breathing device, called the gas mask, was developed by black inventor Garrett Morgan of Cleveland, Ohio. He applied for a patent in 1912. The device was later used for the safety and rescue of trapped coal miners.

46

MORGAN BRINGING FIRST MAN OUT OF TUNNEL

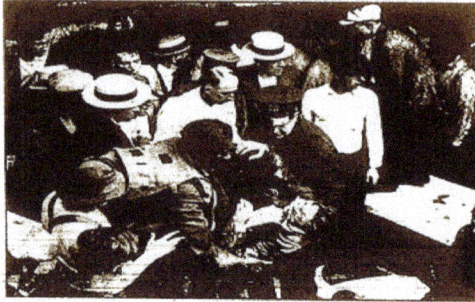

Garrett A. Morgan

Class of 1913

Hettie Sanders
Ethel Harris
Mary Hogans

The fiftieth anniversary of the Emancipation Proclamation was celebrated throughout the nation.

A building in New York City, which in later years became the Apollo Theatre and opened to African-Americans, was built in 1913-14.

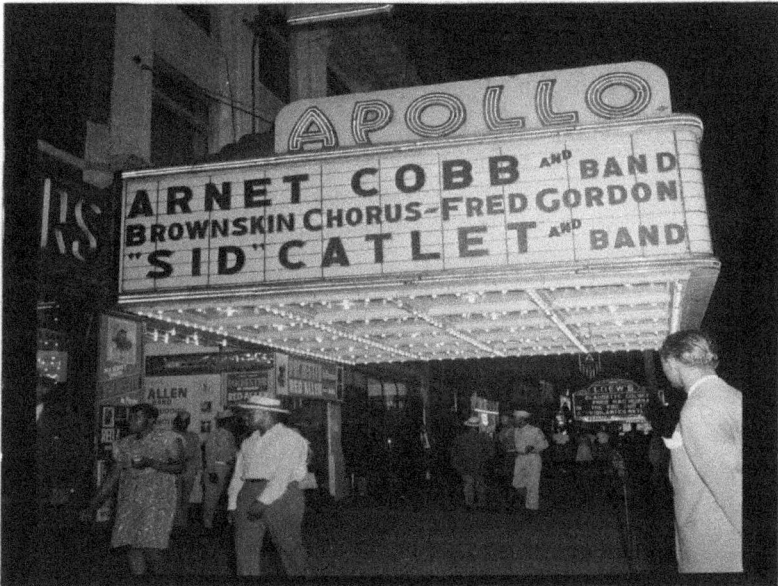

An Apollo Theatre marquee, New York City

Class of 1914

Pasqueline Robinson
Helen Verdier

World War I began in Europe in 1914.

Annette Myers' parents, W. H. and Janie Lang
McCollough, were both Peck High School students.
W.H. McCollough, a 1936 graduate
and in later years known as Captain Mac,
was born at the start of WW1, in 1914.

CLASS OF 1915

GLADYS BRUCE
IRENE EDWARDS
L.B. STAYS
VIVIAN ARCHER

The Singer Sewing Machine rose to popularity in the 1915 era. This antique-style machine is still being used in households around the world today.

49

The author's mother, Janie, was a well-known seamstress in the Fernandina Community using a singer-sewing machine like this one.

CLASS OF 1916

SARAH CRIBB
GLARVEAN MOSELEY
IRENE MERCHANT
HELENA LITTLES
ALLEEN M. COOK

Carter G. Woodson, the father of Black History and Negro History Week, founded the *Journal of Negro History* in 1916.

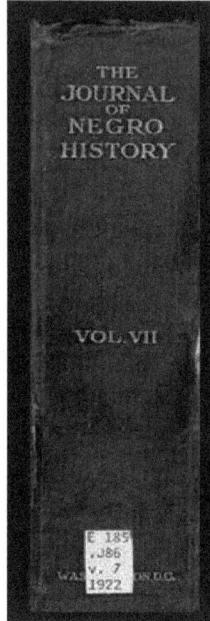

Now called *The Journal of African American History*

1917

African-American singer and actress Lena Horne was born in 1917. She died in 2010.

CLASS OF 1918

FLORIDA COOK

The year marked the end of World War I, which began in 1914 and ended with the Armistice of November 1918.

52

African-Americans fighting in WW1 in 1918, called the Harlem Hellfighters, also referred to as the Black Rattlers and Men of Bronze

CLASS OF 1919

DAISY YOUNG
FAUSTINA CLAY

In 1919, "Lift Every Voice and Sing" was adopted by the NAACP as the "Negro National Anthem."

Lift every voice and sing
Till earth and heaven ring,
Ring with the harm-o-nies of Liberty;
Let our rejoicing rise,
High as the list'ning skies,
Let it resound loud as the rolling sea.
Sing a song full of the faith that the dark past has taught us,
Sing a song full of the hope that the present has brought us,
Facing the rising sun of our new day begun,
Let us march on till victory is won.

Stony the road we trod,
Bitter the chastening rod,
Felt in the days when hope unborn had died;
Yet with a steady beat,
Have not our weary feet
Come to the place for which our fathers sighed?
We have come over a way that with tears has been watered,
We have come treading our path through the blood of the slaughtered,
Out from the gloomy past, till now we stand at last
Where the white gleam of our bright star is cast.

God of our weary years,
God of our silent tears,
Thou who hast brought us thus far on the way;
Thou who has by Thy might
Led us into the light,
Keep us forever in the path, we pray.
Lest our feet stray from the places, our God, where we met Thee,
Lest our hearts, drunk with the wine of the world, we forget Thee,
Shadowed beneath Thy hand, may we forever stand,
True to our God, true to our native land.

53

CLASS OF 1920

WILLIE MCCLEARY
EDDIE PECK
ANNIE COOK

The 1920s began a significant period of creativity for black poets, writers, artists and authors, known as the Harlem Renaissance.

Attire of the 1920s

1921

No Class Recorded

In 1921, Elizabeth "Bessie" Coleman earned her aviation pilot's license. She was the first African-American to receive an international aviation license.

Bessie Coleman and her plane around 1922

55

CLASS OF 1922

HATTIE PECK
ETHEL EVELYN MOSELEY
LOUISE DELANEY

Emma Beard Delaney, missionary to Africa, born in 1871, died in 1922.

William Leo Hansberry of Howard University taught the first known course in African- American history and civilization at an American university.

Julius Rosenwald, of Jewish origin, an acquaintance and admirer of African-American Booker T. Washington of Tuskegee Institute, helped build many schools for African-American children before and during the 1920s, the era when Peck High School was built. Peck is said to be a Rosenwald school. The Rosenwald fund was established by the multimillionaire businessman, one of the founders of Sears, Roebuck, and Company, in 1917. The philanthropist died in 1932.

**Julius Rosenwald with pupils
at one of the schools his fund assisted.**

1923

No Class Recorded

Garrett A. Morgan, African-American inventor, was issued a patent for his three-way automatic traffic light.

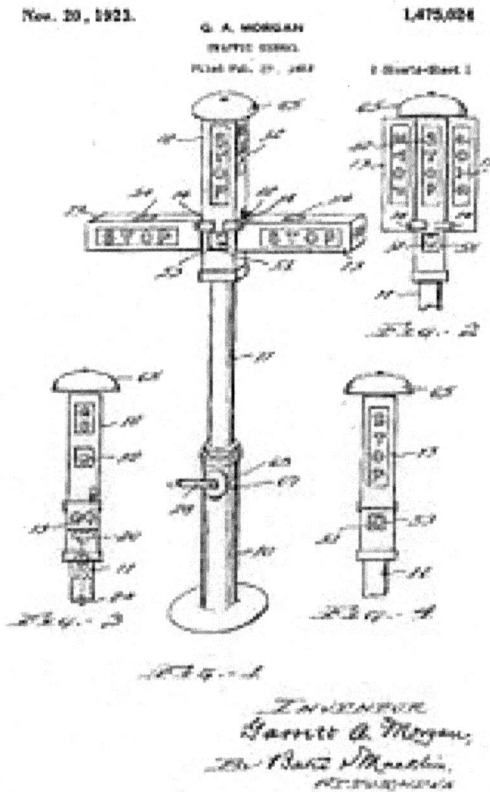

Signal light patent drawing

CLASS OF 1924

EDNA ARLEEN NOBLE
FREDERICA LEONA PINKNEY
SADIE ELIZABETH MCCLEARY
MAMIE CECELIA VERDIER
HARRY THOMAS WILLIAMS
MCKEVER HENRY HUGGINS

Class Motto: *"Age quod agis"*
Class Colors: Purple and Gold
Class Flower: Easter Lily

Mary McLeod Bethune became president of the National Association of Colored Women in 1924, serving until 1928.

CLASS OF 1925

CORA E. PINKNEY
MAMIE V. KEELER
CHARLES H. WILLIAMS
MINOR A. MCCLEARY

Class Motto: *"Vineit qui se vineit"*
Class Colors: Blue and Orange
Class Flower: Rose

Singer Bessie Smith and Louis Armstrong recorded the "St. Louis Blues."

"The Cotton Climate Claims" that later became the Nassau County Branch of the NAACP was founded in 1925 by Brooks Thompson and his daughter Martha Hippard. Thompson, an ex-slave, was also a teacher of carpentry at Peck High School.

59

FLEET OF SHRIMP BOATS AT FERNANDINA, FLA.

Fleet of shrimp boats at Fernandina in the 1920s

1926

No Class Recorded

Negro History Week was founded by Carter G. Woodson. Today, it is celebrated as Black History Month, also known as African-American History Month.

CLASS OF 1927

IRA MAE FREDERICK

Peck High School, built in 1927, stands in the 500th block of Eleventh Street in Fernandina Beach.

The Harlem Globetrotters basketball team was organized in Chicago in January 1927.

Class of 1928

Annie Lucile Foster
Ray Ulysses Noble
Leonard Augustus Ross
Martha Winifred DeLaney
Samuel Vernon Simpson

After many years of experimenting with synchronized sound and film together, the motion picture industry became a new day in sound between 1926 and 1929.

Mickey's first sound track appearance in *Steamboat Willie* (1928)

CLASS OF 1929

EVERLINA LOIS PRICE
MARGARET ELIZABETH QUARTERMAN
WILLIE LEE ELIZABETH BAKER
PEARL PAUTHENIA FREDERICK
HELEN MILDRED EDWARDS
RAYMOND R. ARMSTRONG
ALTON PERCELL BROWN

Class Motto: "We Finish to Begin."
Class Colors: Purple and Amber
Class Flower: White Lily

Due to the stock market crash in the United States, the decade of 1929 through 1939 was the longest economic and Great Depression of all time.

Michael King, Jr., who later became Martin Luther King, Jr., was born in Atlanta, Georgia, in 1929.

63

1930

No Class Recorded

In spite of the "Great Depression," due to the stock market crash, and "Jim Crow" in the 1930s, African-Americans made recognizable advancements in sports, music, education, art and many other areas.

64

Duke Ellington, a famous jazz musician, poses with his piano at the KFG Fitzsimons Army Medical Center's radio station.

CLASS OF 1931

LEONA MILDRED MERRELL
FANNIE MAE PAYNE
OPHELIA HELENA JOHNSON
JAMES BENJAMIN QUARTERMAN
RACHEL PRENELLA VERDIER
JOAN FRANCES GAVIN
HENRY JAMES FLOYD

Class Motto: *"Quid erimus, nune flemus"*
Class Colors: Purple and Gold
Class Flower: Hydrangeas

African-American rock musician Ike Turner was born in 1931 and died in 2007. Also born in 1931 was Toni Morrison, African-American writer and 1993 recipient of the Nobel Prize in Literature.

65

Peck High School for Black students grades 1-12 opened in 1927.

The Faculty, 1931

Peck High School faculty in 1931

(Standing, from left) William H. Peck, Martha De Laney, Helen Argrett, Professor B.F. Hartwell, Elizabeth R. Morrison and Jenkins Morrison; (seated, from left) Laura E. Jones, Maria Edwards Peck, Irene Merchant Colson, Janie F. Taylor, Beulah Dupree and Annie Marie Cook.

"Education is the most powerful weapon which you can use to change the world."

~ Nelson Mandela

Names of African-American educators and staff members up to Peck's closing in 1969

1891-1969

Administration
Teachers
Staff

Some names may have been left out due to lack of
information and unavailable records.
Additional information may be added to the next edition,
upon proof of documentation.

ADMINISTRATION

PRINCIPALS AND ASSISTANT PRINCIPALS (A.P.)

MOSES H. PAYNE
WILLIAM HENDERSON (W.H.) PECK
WILLIAM V. NIXON
T. TILLINGHAST
W.H. BULLOCK
EDYTH J. THURSTON
WILLIAM GREEN
A. QUINN JONES, JR.
JAMES B. BRYANT
ROSCOE WEBB
W. D. HICKS
MAURICE BARNETT
R.T. ANDERSON
JOEMILLS H. BRADDOCK (A.P.)
NATHANIEL L. HANKERSON (A.P.)
ALBERT J. WILLIAMS (A.P.)

EARLY YEARS

MRS. A.E. DUHART (A.P.)
RUBY G. HARGRETT (A.P.)

EARLY GOLDEN ERA TEACHERS

MISS J.L. ELLERBE

IDELLA L. PINKNEY

FLORIDA DEAS

JANIE F. TAYLOR

MRS. R.H. COWAN

BELLE TRENT JORDAN

MISS A.L. BURNETT

MARIA EDWARDS PECK

MARY R. BAKER

HELEN MARTIN

BROOKS THOMPSON

REV. E.A. SIMMONS

LAURA E. JONES

ERNISTINE VIERO

EDWINA P. NICHOLS

MARTHA W. DELANEY

BEULAH M. DE LORME DUPREE

ELIZABETH R. MORRISON

ALLEEN COOK BRADLEY

MINNIE L. HAWKINS

PROFESSOR B.F. HARTWELL

HELEN ARGRETT

IRENE MERCHANT COLSON

ANNIE MARIE COOK

JENKINS MORRISON

TEACHERS

CHARLES L. ALBERT, JR.
GENE ARLINE
WILLIE MAE ASHLEY
CHRISTINE W. BLUE
ALTAMESE BROOKS
ALICE B. CARD
MS. CARNEGIE
PAULINE STATEN CHEESE
NATHALIE CLEMONS
DAISY D. COAKLEY
JOHNNIE COWART
DELORES CRENSHAW
DANIEL RAY DELANEY
JOHN DEMPS
JOSHUA K. DOVE
NETTIE COOK DOVE
EMMA L. FEACHER
JOHNNIE MAXINE FISHER
MINNIE P. GADLING
FLORIDA ROBINSON GARDNER
MILDRED GARDNER
CALVIN GIBBS
MINNIE T. GLOSTER
MS. GRUNDY
MRS. HANSBERRY
JAMES HAYES
WILLIE MAE MYERS SLAUGHTER-HICKS
BEATRICE WOODARD HILL
FRANCES HOLLIDAY
HORACE HOLLIDAY
HERBERT HOUSTON
WILLIAM JACKSON
FRANCENA L. MORRISON JACOBS

CAROLYN JAMES
THELMA BROOKINS JOHNSON
EARL JONES
GLOVINE JONES
MAMIE JORDAN
CORINNE M. KENNEDY
STANLEY F. LOFTON
ROBERT MANNING
LUCY MAE MATTHEW
RUTH McCASKILL
WILLIE McCOY
KATHERINE B. McKINNEY
SARAH G. McWHITE
LEROY MIDDLETON
EDWIN MORGAN
ANNETTE McCOLLOUGH MYERS
FRANK OWENS
MARTHA OWENS
CLARA DUHART PATTERSON
MS. E.D. PATTERSON
ESTHER MAE PERSON
RAMONA PINKNEY
EDWIN PLEASANT
MR. POLLARD
FERRIS RHODES
WILLIE MAE RILEY
JOHNNIE L. ROBINSON
DAVE ROGERS
EUGENE F. SCOTT
MARIE TRAEYE SCOTT
THELMA SHEPPARD
RUTH SIKES
CLARENCE M. SIMMONS
ELEANOR SIMMONS
EARL B. SIMPSON
JOHNNY T. SMITH
MR./MS. SOLOMON

71

Rufus Sullivan
Synetta Taylor
Irma Villarin Telfair
Edythe J. Thurston
Flora Lee Redmon Tyler
Johnnie Mae Vann
Josephine Ware
Albert J. Williams
Betty Gilbert Williams
Georgia M. Sheffield Williams
Jimmye Owens Williams
Margaret Simmons Williams
Miller N. Williams
Nelson Williams
Eugene Albert, Joe Lee Smith (Interns)

STAFF

Front Office, Cafeteria Management, Visiting Teachers,
Substitute Teachers,
Custodians, Bus Drivers, etc.

RUTH BELL PERSON MORGAN
School Secretary and Interim Administrator

VERNITA JOHNSON HOLMES
Cafeteria Manager

JESSIE HARKER JACKSON
VIOLA BALL
REBECCA FOSTER
DOLLIE HARDEN
LOTTIE COOK WILLIAMS
WILLIAM MCCAUGLE
ERNESTINE BOONE
JAMES "BUCK" COOPER
ALEXANDER C. HILL
EVERLENA W. MORRIS HILLERY
GERALDINE HIGDON
ROY T. TERRY, JR.
ANDREW GRANT
JOSEPH RICHO
CLAUDIA SOLOMON
REV. L.S. MORRISON
REV. JAMES P. ALLEN – TRUANT OFFICER

73

Historic Images
and Documents Gallery

William H. Peck Headstone
Peck Marker
Peck High School Building Plaque

New Zion (Missionary) Baptist Church Marker
History of New Zion (Missionary) Baptist Church
Photographs of Father Lewis Cook in His Earlier Years

Former Peck Home Site

Nassau County Courthouse
Graduation Programs – Classes 1924-1931
United States (Fernandina Beach) Post Office

United States Colored Troops (USCT) Headstones

Emancipation Proclamation
History of NCCDC
Peck High Alma Mater

PHOTOS BY ANGELA DAUGHTRY/NEWS-LEADER

James "Mickey" Mullen, a 1956 Peck graduate, and E. Veronica Pace place a wreath May 1, 2009, at the William H. Peck headstone, established by Ms. Pace in 2008, to honor the memory of her great-grandfather at Bosque Bello Cemetery in Fernandina.

PECK HIGH SCHOOL
PRINCIPAL

WILLIAM H. PECK
APRIL 18, 1859
AUGUST 28, 1950

ELDER
TRINITY M.E. CHURCH

Professor Peck is buried alongside his third wife, Maria McHenry Edwards Peck (1888-1968), a Peck teacher, whom he married in 1931. His second wife, Georgia Mordecai Peck (1864-1927), whom he married in 1891, is also buried in Bosque Bello Cemetery.

Peck Marker – Side 1
unveiled February 20, 2016

78

PECK HIGH SCHOOL

(Continued from other side)

As one of the oldest African American high schools in the state, Peck High School was the center of the African American community and a source of pride. Used for classes in the day, the school served as a meeting place for community groups in the evening. In later years, adult education and industrial skills were also offered. Teachers were an integral part of the fabric of the community and embraced their roles with great pride and commitment, understanding that they were educating students, families, and a community. When schools in Fernandina were desegregated in 1969, Peck was closed. Students were integrated into other schools and by 1976 the building was vacant. Recognizing the impact the deteriorating building had on the spirit of an entire community, a diverse group including Ellie Colburn, Elmo Myers, Charles Albert, and Willie Mae Ashley began the campaign to save Peck High in the 1990s, state grants and the City of Fernandina Beach funded its restoration, and it reopened as the Peck Center. The center houses non-profit groups, city offices, and hosts recreational activities and special events, making it possible for Peck to celebrate its past while continuing to serve the community.

A FLORIDA HERITAGE SITE
SPONSORED BY PECK ALUMNI ASSOCIATION, CITY OF FERNANDINA BEACH, AND THE FLORIDA DEPARTMENT OF STATE

79

Peck Marker – Side 2
February 20, 2016

80

Peck High School Building Plaque

New Zion (Missionary) Baptist Church marker
unveiled November 18, 2001

History of New Zion
(Missionary) Baptist Church

New Zion Missionary Baptist Church is the second oldest and largest Black Missionary Baptist Church on Amelia Island. The church had its beginning on May 15, 1870, under the leadership of Rev. Lewis Cook, a pioneer of the gospel, with sixty-nine followers who came out of the First Baptist Church to extend kingdom-building. Their first meeting was held in a stable on First Street, followed by meetings in various homes, while still seeking a permanent place of worship. The first conference after organizing was held in the home of Sister Elsie Knabb. Rev. Potter, moderator of the First Bethlehem Baptist Association, presided over the meeting. Testing their strengths and efforts, Rev. Potter gave the parishioners six months to build.

Those sixty-nine parishioners, ably supported by Father Cook (as he was called), purchased the land for the church on Tenth Street and Atlantic Avenue on April 1, 1878. Within six months, the original wooden church was erected on the present site known as Lot 1 – Block 53.

How happy the devout Christians were, saying, "What shall we name this place of worship?" Sister Dinah Brown said, "Call her *New Zion* and she will never grow old." Many souls were added to the church during the pastorate of Reverend Cook, founder and builder. After ten years of service as pastor, God called Father Cook from labor to reward on October 1, 1880. Six pastors served from 1870 to 1902.

On January 6, 1904, Rev. P.A. Callaham, BD (Bachelor of Divinity) of South Carolina was called. Unfortunately, the original church building was destroyed by fire February

11, 1907. The task of rebuilding the walls of the church became a challenge. Rev. Callaham immediately formed a building committee composed of himself, Deacons William Flowers, Harper Cook, John Horn and others. By a vote of the conference, a brick church was ordered and erected. The task of building a new church became a challenge under the skillful guidance of William "Billy" Rivers, a local well-known black contractor and boat- and ship-builder. Under Rivers' guidance, the church is built in the shape of an upside-down ship. The present beautiful brick structure, built on the same site as the original church, was erected by November 1907. In the erection of the new church, Rev. Callaham can be easily styled as the master builder with oneness and unity among his followers. The cornerstone was laid in 1907. The members continued to work under various pastors. Within six years (in 1912), under the leadership of Rev. J.N. Stokes, the mortgage on the church, pews, etc., was burned, with one of the sixty-nine parishioners, Sister Margaret Popena, holding the mortgage as it burned.

There have been many accomplishments of this historic church under the leadership of twenty-two pastors up to 2016.

Through the years, other preachers who helped bridge the gap between appointed pastors were Rev. Gus Clemon (G.C.) Bradley of Fernandina and Rev. Lenworth S. (L.S.) Morrison of O'Neil, Florida. For many years, Deacons Seth Mitchell and John Mitchell (no kin) served as bell tower ringers.

On December 7, 1997, installation services were held for Pastor Reverend Jeremiah Robinson, Jr., of Jacksonville, Florida. Pastor Robinson and Sister Cynthia Robinson and their family have been a blessing to the New Zion family.

Two state-funded matching grants were written by Sister Annette Myers and awarded by the State of Florida in 2000. Steered by committee members and the pastor, both grants were successfully administered and completed in 2001: namely, a historic preservation survey of the exterior façade of the church, and a state marker placed at the church site with assistance from the City of Fernandina Beach and approved by the local Historic Preservation Council. The historic stained-glass Queen Anne windows and other windows of the church were all restored back to their original state in 2007. On Sunday, March 25, 2007, a dedication service was held in celebration of the completion of the window restoration project.

Over the years, our community has benefited from having New Zion Missionary Baptist Church, where Peck High graduations and other activities have been held. Today, historic New Zion still serves the community through its outreach ministries, annual Martin Luther King, Jr., Commemorative Services, a partner with the State of Florida (Access Florida) in their food stamps, cash assistance and Medicaid programs, and in many other beautiful ways.

84

New Zion Missionary Baptist Church has been a beacon light contributing her share of Christian development and expansion to the local community, state and nation and remains a significant landmark in the historic district of Fernandina Beach.

Photographs of Reverend Lewis Cook in his earlier years.
He was later referred to as "Father Cook"
by his parishioners.
1834-1880
Buried in Bosque Bello Cemetery

This large live oak tree stands on the site where Professor Peck's home was located on Ash Street in Fernandina Beach. The property now is occupied by Super Dollar store. The historic tree is still there.

Nassau County Courthouse, built in 1891

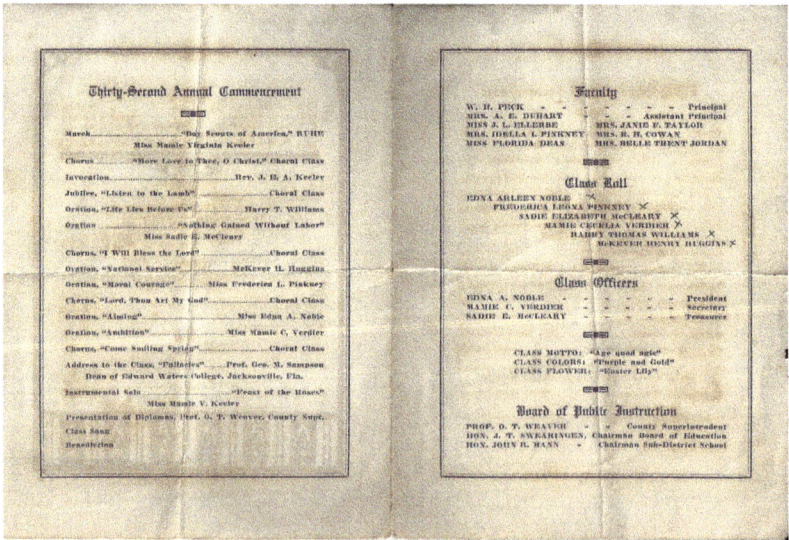

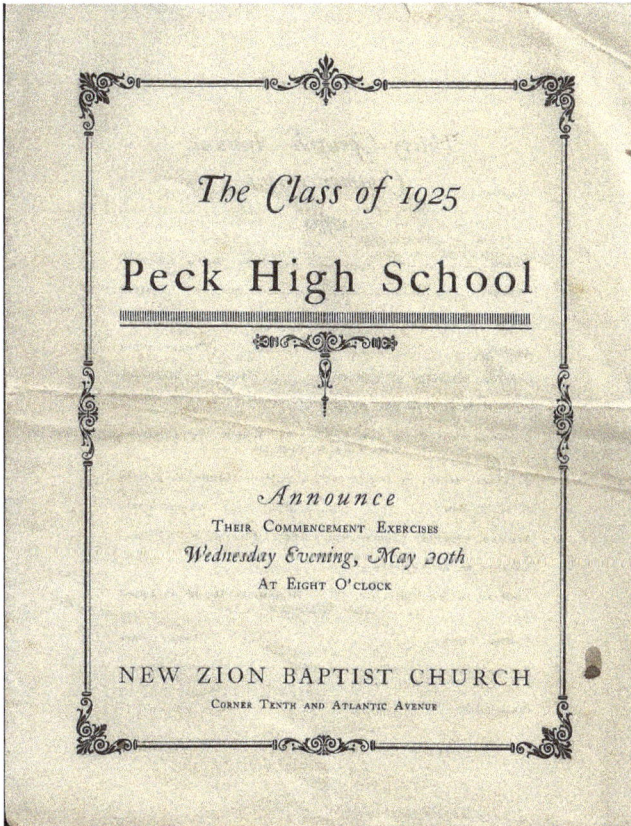

The Class of 1925

Peck High School

Announce

THEIR COMMENCEMENT EXERCISES

Wednesday Evening, May 20th

AT EIGHT O'CLOCK

NEW ZION BAPTIST CHURCH

CORNER TENTH AND ATLANTIC AVENUE

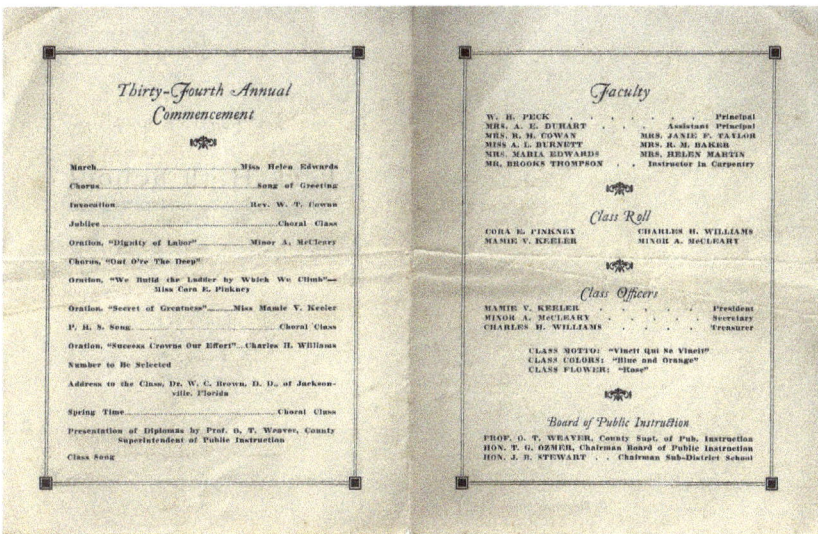

Thirty-Fourth Annual Commencement

March .... Miss Helen Edwards

Chorus .... Song of Greeting

Invocation .... Rev. W. T. Cowan

Jubilee .... Choral Class

Oration, "Dignity of Labor" .... Minor A. McCleary

Chorus, "Out O're The Deep"

Oration, "We Build the Ladder by Which We Climb"— Miss Cora E. Pinkney

Oration, "Secret of Greatness" .... Miss Mamie V. Keeler

P. H. S. Song .... Choral Class

Oration, "Success Crowns Our Effort" .. Charles H. Williams

Number to Be Selected

Address to the Class, Dr. W. C. Brown, D. D., of Jacksonville, Florida

Spring Time .... Choral Class

Presentation of Diplomas by Prof. O. T. Weaver, County Superintendent of Public Instruction

Class Song

Faculty

W. H. PECK .... Principal
MRS. A. E. DUHART .... Assistant Principal
MRS. R. M. COWAN   MRS. JANIE F. TAYLOR
MISS A. L. BURNETT   MRS. R. M. BAKER
MRS. MARIA EDWARDS   MRS. HELEN MARTIN
MR. BROOKS THOMPSON ...... Instructor in Carpentry

Class Roll

CORA E. PINKNEY   CHARLES H. WILLIAMS
MAMIE V. KEELER   MINOR A. McCLEARY

Class Officers

MAMIE V. KEELER .... President
MINOR A. McCLEARY .... Secretary
CHARLES H. WILLIAMS .... Treasurer

CLASS MOTTO: "Vincit Qui Se Vincit"
CLASS COLORS: "Blue and Orange"
CLASS FLOWER: "Rose"

Board of Public Instruction

PROF. O. T. WEAVER, County Supt. of Pub. Instruction
HON. T. G. OZMER, Chairman Board of Public Instruction
HON. J. B. STEWART . . Chairman Sub-District School

THE CLASS OF 1927

Peck High School

A N N O U N C E

THEIR COMMENCEMENT EXERCISES

Wednesday Evening, May 18th

At Eight O'clock

NEW ZION BAPTIST CHURCH

Corner Tenth and Atlantic Avenue

Thirty-Sixth Annual Commencement

Processional

Chorus .... "Evening Shadows"

Invocation .... Dr. J. B. L. Williams, D. D.

Chorus .... "Jubilee"

Oration, "Labor" .... Miss Ira Mae Frederick

Chorus .... "Over The Waves We Softly Glide"

Presentation of Speaker, Dr. T. W. Carter, B. D., Dean
of Theology, of Edward Waters College
By Rev. E. A. Simmons

Chorus .... "Fond Lillies"

Presentation of Diploma by Prof. O. T. Weaver, Supt.
of Public Instruction

Solo .... By Miss Ira Mae Frederick

Chorus .... "Our Last Goodbye"

Faculty

PROF. W. H. PECK, Principal
MRS. RUBY HARGRETT, Assistant Principal
REV. E. A. SIMMONS   MRS. JANIE F. TAYLOR
MRS. L. E. JONES   MRS. EDWINA P. NICHOLS
MRS. MARIA EDWARDS MRS. HELEN V. MARTIN
MRS. R. M. BAKER, Teacher in Domestic Science
MRS. ERNISTINE VIERO, Instructor in Dressmaking
MR. BROOK THOMPSON, Instructor in Carpentry

CLASS ROLL

MISS IRA MAE FREDERICK

CLASS MOTTO: .... "Labor Omnia Vincit"
CLASS COLORS: .... Gold and White
CLASS FLOWER: .... White Rose

BOARD OF PUBLIC INSTRUCTION

PROF. O. T. WEAVER
Superintendent of Public Instruction

HON. T. G. OZMER
Chairman of Board of Public Instruction

SENATOR J. H. STEWART
Chairman of Sub-District School Board

Thirty-Seventh Annual /1928
Commencement

❦

Procession	Miss Edwina M. Peck
Invocation	Rev. E. A. Cook
Chorus	"Come To The Gay Feast Of Song"
Salutatory Oration	"Self Reliance"
	Miss Annie Lucile Foster
Oration	"Aiming"
	Ray Ulysses Noble
Chorus	"By The Waters Of Minnetonka"
Oration	"Excelsior"
	Leonard Augustus Ross
Oration	"The Necessity Of A Definite Aim"
	Miss Martha Winifred DeLaney
Instrumental Solo	Miss Edwina M. Peck
Valedictory Address	"The Survival Of The Fittest"
	Samuel Vernon Simpson
Chorus	"A Song Of Spring"

Presentation of Speaker, Dr. J. R. E. Lee, President of F.
A. and M. College of Tallahassee, Fla.
By Rev. E. A. Simmons

Chorus	"In Old Madrid"
Presentation of Diplomas	Prof. O. T. Weaver
	Superintendent of Public Instruction
Class Song.	

91

The Graduating Class
of the
Peck High School
requests your presence at its
Commencement Exercises
on Wednesday evening, the fifth of June
at eight o'clock
New Zion Baptist Church
Corner Tenth and Center Streets
Fernandina, Florida

Class Motto:
WE FINISH TO BEGIN

Class Colors:
PURPLE AND AMBER

Class Flower:
WHITE LILY

Class Roll:
EVERLENA LOIS PRICE
MARGARET ELIZABETH QUARTERMAN
WILLIE LEE ELIZABETH BAKER
PEARL PAUTHENIA FREDERICK
HELEN MILDRED EDWARDS
RAYMOND R. ARMSTRONG
ALTON PERCELL BROWN

W. H. PECK, Principal
O. T. WEAVER, Superintendent

1891   1931

The Senior Class

of

Peck High School

invites you to be present at their

Commencement Exercises

Wednesday evening, May twentieth, nineteen hundred thirty-one

eight o'clock

New Zion Baptist Church

Corner Center and Tenth Streets

1891   1931

PROGRAM

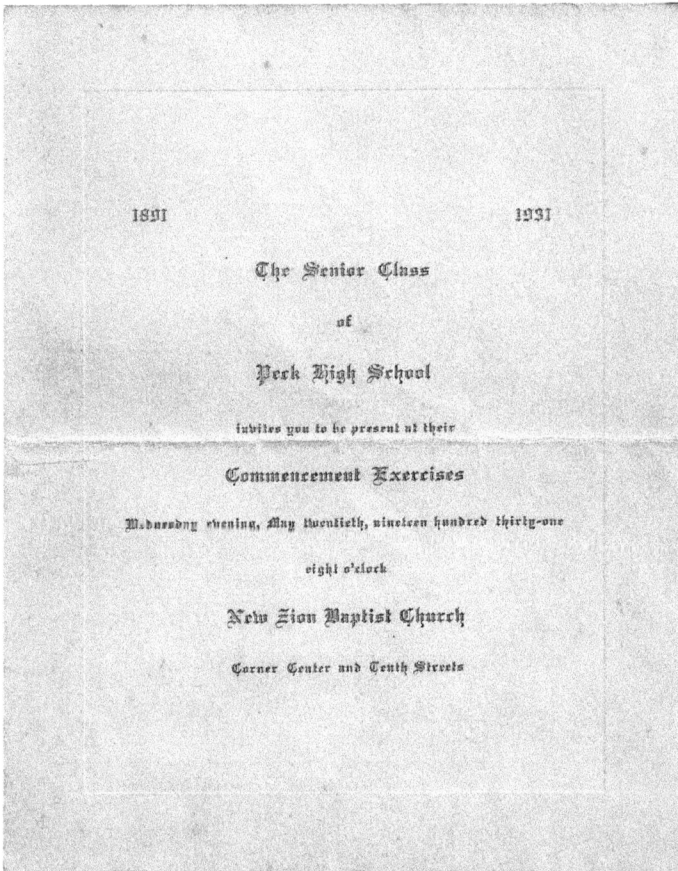

FORTIETH ANNUAL COMMENCEMENT
PECK HIGH SCHOOL
PROCESSIONAL

Chorus—"Over the Waves We Softly Glide"
Invocation _____ Rev. L. S. Morrison
Chorus—"Trees"
Salutatory—"Beyond the Clouds the Sun Still Shines"
       Miss Fannie Mae Payne
Class History _____ Miss Ophelia Helena Johnson
Class Prophet _____ Miss Leona Mildred Merrell
Class Poem _____ Miss Rachel Prenella Verdier
Class Will _____ Mr. James Benjamin Quarterman
Chorus—"Out Over the Deep"
Valedictory—"Row Though the Tide Be Against You"
       Miss Joan Francis Gavin
Quartetto—"When Dawn Breaks Through"
Address _____ Rev. A. W. Puller, D.D., LL.D.
Chorus—"Carmena"
Presentation of Diplomas ___ Hon. A. W. Jackson, County Supt.
Acceptance of Diplomas _____ Mr. Henry James Floyd

Class Motto: Quid erimus, nunc flemus
Class Colors: Purple and Gold
Class Flower: Hydrangeas

CLASS ROLL

Leona Mildred Merrell
Fannie Mae Payne
Ophelia Helena Johnson
James Benjamin Quarterman
Rachel Prenella Verdier
Joan Frances Gavin
Henry James Floyd

FACULTY

Miss Martha W. De Laney
Miss Beaulah M. De Lorme
Mrs. Irene E. Brown
Mrs. Janie F. Taylor
Mrs. Laura E. Jones
Miss Annie M. Cook
Mrs. Maria E. Peck
Mrs. Elizabeth R. Morrison
Mrs. Minnie L. Hawkins
Mrs. Ruby G. Hargrett
Prof. B. F. Hartwell
W. H. Peck, Principal

94

United States (Fernandina Beach) Post Office,
completed in 1912

Jefferson Harris
headstone, 1832-1888

Jonas Miller headstone,
date of birth and date
of death unknown

95

The American Civil War — 1861-1865
Union Soldiers buried in Bosque Bello Cemetery

Discovery has been made that there are other United States Colored Troops (USCT), African-American gravesites in Bosque Bello Cemetery, but time has rotted their wood grave markers. According to President Abraham Lincoln, "Without the military help of the black freedmen, the war against the South could not have been won." It is also declared that without the Emancipation Proclamation, the USCT soldiers and sailors would have had little or no reason to fight for the Union. It has been suggested that these brave men of war might be ancestors of some members of the Peck alumni.

THE EMANCIPATION PROCLAMATION

By the President of the United States of America:
A Proclamation.

*W*hereas, on the twenty-second day of September, in the year of our Lord one thousand eight hundred and sixty-two, a proclamation was issued by the President of the United States, containing, among other things, the following, to wit:

"That on the first day of January, in the year of our Lord one thousand eight hundred and sixty-three, all persons held as slaves within any State or designated part of a State, the people whereof shall then be in rebellion against the United States, shall be then, thenceforward, and forever free; and the Executive Government of the United States, including the military and naval authority thereof, will recognize and maintain the freedom of such persons, and will do no act or acts to repress such persons, or any of them, in any efforts they may make for their actual freedom.

96

"That the Executive will, on the first day of January aforesaid, by proclamation, designate the States and parts of States, if any, in which the people thereof, respectively, shall then be in rebellion against the United States; and the fact that any State, or the people thereof, shall on that day be, in good faith, represented in the Congress of the United States by members chosen thereto at elections wherein a majority of the qualified voters of such State shall have participated, shall, in the absence of strong countervailing testimony, be deemed conclusive evidence that such State, and the people thereof, are not then in rebellion against the United States."

Now, therefore I, Abraham Lincoln, President of the United States, by virtue of the power in me vested as Commander-in-Chief, of the Army and Navy of the United States in time of actual armed rebellion against the authority and government of the United States, and as a fit and necessary war measure for suppressing said rebellion, do, on this first day of January, in the year of our Lord one thousand eight hundred and sixty-three, and in accordance with my purpose so to do publicly proclaimed for the full period of one hundred days, from the day first above mentioned, order and designate as the States and parts of States wherein the people thereof respectively, are this day in rebellion against the United States, the following, to wit:

Arkansas, Texas, Louisiana, (except the Parishes of St. Bernard, Plaquemines, Jefferson, St. John, St.Charles, St. James Ascension, Assumption, Terrebonne, Lafourche, St. Mary, St. Martin, and Orleans, including the City of New Orleans) Mississippi, Alabama, Florida, Georgia, South Carolina, North Carolina, and Virginia, (except the forty-eight counties designated as West Virginia, and also the counties of Berkley, Accomac, Northampton, Elizabeth City, York, Princess Ann, and Norfolk, including the cities of Norfolk and Portsmouth), and which excepted parts, are for the present, left precisely as if this proclamation were not issued.

And by virtue of the power, and for the purpose aforesaid, I do order and declare that all persons held as slaves within said designated States, and parts of States, are, and henceforward shall be free; and that the

Executive government of the United States, including the military and naval authorities thereof, will recognize and maintain the freedom of said persons.

And I hereby enjoin upon the people so declared to be free to abstain from all violence, unless in necessary self-defence; and I recommend to them that, in all cases when allowed, they labor faithfully for reasonable wages.

And I further declare and make known, that such persons of suitable condition, will be received into the armed service of the United States to garrison forts, positions, stations, and other places, and to man vessels of all sorts in said service.

And upon this act, sincerely believed to be an act of justice, warranted by the Constitution, upon military necessity, I invoke the considerate judgment of mankind, and the gracious favor of Almighty God.

In witness whereof, I have hereunto set my hand and caused the seal of the United States to be affixed.

Done at the City of Washington, this first day of January, in the year of our Lord one thousand eight hundred and sixty three, and of the Independence of the United States of America the eighty-seventh.

By the President: ABRAHAM LINCOLN

WILLIAM H. SEWARD, Secretary of State.

ABOUT THE
NASSAU COUNTY
COMMUNITY DEVELOPMENT
CORPORATION

*O*n Tuesday, July 31, 1979, a group of concerned citizens met at the local Elm Street Recreation Center for the purpose of airing their grievances over the way the abandoned old Peck High School was being kept and that its appearance presented an eyesore to the community. After integration, the Peck building eventually was no longer useful as a community school.

The group of citizens who met felt that the building should be restored and used to benefit the children and citizens of the community.

The group later agreed upon attorney Walter Kyle of Jacksonville to be their legal advisor, and Kyle accepted their offer. They called themselves the Nassau County Community Development Corporation (NCCDC).

The corporation decided to formulate a charter organization to handle the Peck issue plus other related problems for the betterment of the general Nassau County community. In the early 1980s, attorney Arthur L. "Buddy" Jacobs also became one of the corporation's legal advisors.

The NCCDC, a non-profit organization, was issued a charter on September 21, 1979, by the state of Florida.
Charter members of the corporation were Elmo Myers, Donald Stewart, Beverly Hall, Lewis Faison, Francis Mote,

Annette Myers, Glynn Pope, Vernon Simpson, Reverend Robert Flagler, and John Baker. Elmo Myers was selected to serve as president and agent. Other members who later joined and remained with the corporation were Willie Mae Ashley, Esther M. Person, Margaret Williams and Rufus Johnson.

Upon the loss by the untimely death of outstanding leader Elmo Myers in 1987, Francis Mote became president. Due to the untimely death of Francis Mote in 1994, Glynn Pope began serving as acting president, followed by Annette Myers.

Through the years, the NCCDC worked diligently in the interest of Peck by sponsoring the 1983 and 1985 grand reunions and various community projects to stimulate interest in the preservation of Peck High School.

Four scholarships, the Elmo Myers Memorial Scholarship, the William H. Peck Memorial Scholarship, the NCCDC General Scholarship and the Rychard-Lottie-Annie Cook-Scholarship, are available annually to high school graduating seniors throughout Nassau County.

In 1989, the City of Fernandina Beach acquired the Peck facility from the Nassau County School Board. Renovations began in 1995. The City held a ground-breaking ceremony on August 24, 1996, and the facility is now being utilized. The Northeast Community Action Agency was the first tenant to be housed in the building by the NCCDC. Today, there are various organizations housed in the building. There is a library that is open to the community.

NOTES

The NCCDC is the grassroots organization, under the leadership of Elmo Myers, that kept the City of Fernandina Beach from bulldozing Peck High School when it became abandoned.

On September 21, 1998, a reception was held by the city to dedicate three downstairs rooms in the Peck Center, one for Elmo Myers, president and founder of the NCCDC. In the year 2000, the auditorium was completely restored and chairs dedicated. On December 5, 2002, the City of Fernandina Beach Peck Committee, chaired by Ele Colborn, held a Chamber of Commerce Business After Hours to celebrate the completion of the Peck Center. The Peck Auditorium was renamed in honor of Willie Mae Hardy Ashley on March 6, 2004. The Peck Community Center, including its grounds and buildings, as approved by city commissioners on September 7, 2010, is now a part of the Fernandina Beach Historic District. The NCCDC is appreciative to the City of Fernandina Beach for preserving the historic facility that once served African-American students.

101

**Elmo V. Myers
President, founder,
and agent, NCCDC**

PECK HIGH
(Alma Mater)

Words and Arrangement by Rychard Samuell Cook, II
Class of 1951

PECK HIGH, PECK HIGH, OH AS THE YEARS DRIFT BY
WE DRIFT YES WE DRIFT TOO
PECK HIGH, PECK HIGH
YOU MAKE THE RAIN CLOUDS BLUE
PECK HIGH WE DO LOVE YOU
WE LOVE YOU FOR THE BLESSED THINGS YOU TEACH,
THE DREAMS YOU MAKE COME TRUE
THE RULE THAT SAYS
TO PRACTICE WHAT YOU PREACH
AND YOU'LL COME SMIL-ING THROUGH
PECK HIGH, PECK HIGH
AS LONG AS GOD PRE-VAILS
AS LONG AS LIPS CAN PRAY
THY BLUE AND GOLD
THY BLUE AND GOLD WILL SAIL
ALWAYS OLD PAL ALWAYS

Rychard Samuell Cook passed away on July 19, 2016, in Orlando, Florida, at the age of eighty-three. His funeral services and burial were held in Miami on July 23, 2016.

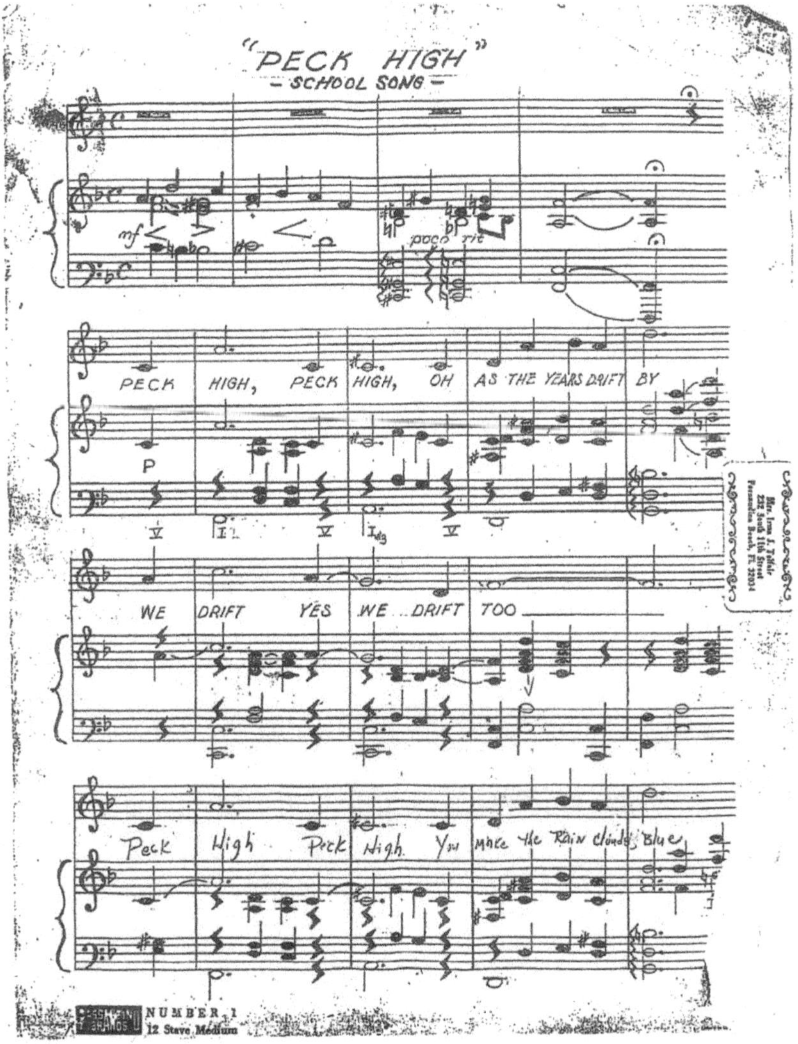

Sheet Music Courtesy of Dave Thompson

ATTRIBUTIONS AND HISTORICAL FACTS

Sources of historical facts and other information in this book were compiled from various resources to include, but not limited to: the internet, historical African-American calendars, Wikipedia.com, *Encyclopedia Britannica*, History.com, *Fernandina Observer*, *Fernandina Beach News-Leader*, Bosque Bello Cemetery records, Amelia Island Museum of History and otherwise where credit is attributed.

Note: Updates or other information, upon proper documentation, may be included in a second edition.

**In later years, Peck High School
adopted the wolf as its mascot.**

Photo Credits

Pg 10 – Fernandina, Florida. Courtesy State Archives of Florida.

Pg 21 – New Zion (Missionary) Baptist Church. Annette Myers.

Pg 22 – Peck gymnasium. Annette Myers.

Pg 23 – Peck buildings circa 1956. From the private collection of Annette Myers.

Pg 24 – Peck Center sign. Annette Myers.

Pg 26 – via Shutterstock.com

Pg 27 – Trinity United Methodist Church. Annette Myers.

Pg 28 - By Sarah Boone, inventors.about.com/library/inventors/blboone.htm, Public Domain, commons.wikimedia.org/w/index.php?curid=17337927

Pg 29 - Daniel Hale Williams. Pre-1923 photograph, Public Domain Source now defunct; image fetched from the Wayback Machine. Description page at [1]. Image at [2]., Public Domain, commons.wikimedia.org/w/index.php?curid=1326189

Pg 30 – Sixth Street. State Archives of Florida

Pg 31 – Buckeye gasoline buggy. By Walter Lewis, photographer, John William Lambert family photos, Wikimedia Commons, Public Domain, commons.wikimedia.org/w/index.php?curid=5464366

Pg 32 – New Zion Baptist Church. The Florida Times-Union, Nassau Neighbor, May 4, 2005.

Pg 33 – Train depot. Annette Myers.

Pg 34 – Rosamond and James Johnson. By Benlabine44, Own work, CC BY-SA 4.0, commons.wikimedia.org/w/index.php?curid=45107448, Photographed by ASCAP

Pg 35 – Afro-American Life Insurance Company. Courtesy Eartha M.M. White Collection, University of North Florida, Thomas G. Carpenter Library (Special Collections and Archives)

Pg 36 – Lumber dock. State Archives of Florida.

Pg 37 – Harriet Tubman. State Archives of Florida.

Pg 38 – Mary McLeod Bethune. State Archives of Florida.

Pg 39 – Clock. Annette Myers.

Pg 41 – New Zion. Courtesy Suzanne Davis Hardee.

Pg 42 – Classroom. www.britannica.com/topic/education/images-videos/African-American-school-near-Henderson-Ky/120015

Pg 43 – NAACP emblem. Fair use.

Pg 44 – Magazine. By W.E.B. DuBois, original book, Public Domain, commons.wikimedia.org/w/index.php?curid=207530

Pg 45 – Great-granddaughter of Professor Peck. Fernandina Beach News-Leader, August 19, 2005

Pg 46 – Coal miner rescue. PD-1923, Public Domain, commons.wikimedia.org/w/index.php?curid=5796155

Pg 46 – Garrett A. Morgan. Public Domain,en.wikipedia.org/w/index.php?curid=9611460

Pg 47 – Apollo Theater marquee. By William P. Gottlieb - lcweb2.loc.gov/diglib/ihas/loc.natlib.gottlieb.00141/enlarge.html?page=1&section=ver01&size=1024&from=, Public Domain, https://commons.wikimedia.org/w/index.php?curid=11224500

Pg 49 – Singer sewing machine. CC BY-SA 2.0, commons.wikimedia.org/w/index.php?curid=657499

Pg 50 – Journal of Negro History. By Association for the Study of African American Life and History, (Life time: none) Original publication: published in New York. Immediate source: en.wikipedia.org/wiki/The_Journal_of_African_American_History

Pg 51 – Lena Horne. By Friedman-Abeles, New York, photographer. Public Domain, commons.wikimedia.org/w/index.php?curid=16738351

Pg 52 – War painting. Public Domain,en.wikipedia.org/w/index.php?curid=1533115

Pg 54 – Attire of the 1920s. Courtesy Donald and Dedria Myers.

106

Pg 55 – Bessie Coleman. By Unknown, www.ctie.monash.edu.au, Public Domain, commons.wikimedia.org/w/index.php?curid=23091723

Pg 56 – Julius Rosenwald and pupils. Fisk University, John Hope and Aurelia E. Franklin Library

Pg 57 – Signal patent. Public Domain, en.wikipedia.org/w/index.php?curid=9610200

Pg 58 – Mary McLeon Bethune. State Archives of Florida.

Pg 59 – Fleet of shrimp boats. State Archives of Florida.

Pg 60 – Logo. Public Domain, Department of Defense

Pg 61 – Peck High School. Annette Myers.

Pg 62 – Steamboat Willie. Copyright MCMXXIX (1929) DISNEY, Fair use, en.wikipedia.org/w/index.php?curid=2657246

Pg 63 – Martin Luther King, Jr. Public Domain, Department of Defense.

Pg 64 – Duke Ellington. www.defenseimagery.mil; VIRIN: HA-SN-99-00410 (cropped), Public Domain, commons.wikimedia.org/w/index.php?curid=8378297

Pg 76 – James "Mickey" Mullen. *Fernandina Beach News-Leader*, May 29, 2009.

Pg 77 – Gravestone. Findagrave.com; added by MaLisa Fender Rembowski.

Pg 78-81 – Peck High School markers. Annette Myers.

Pg 85 – Father Lewis Cook. Photos courtesy of Narvea Clem Gardner, son of Florida Robinson Gardner.

Pg 86 – Live oak. Annette Myers.

Pg 87 – Courthouse. Annette Myers.

Pg 94 – Post office. Annette Myers.

Pg 95 – Gravestones. findagrave.com, added by Chris Belcher (Jefferson Harris headstone), 1832-1888 and findagrave.com, added by MaLisa Fender Rembowski (Jonas Miller headstone).

Pg 109 – via Shutterstock.com

OTHER BOOKS OF RELATED INTEREST

Tidewater Amelia
Jan H. Johannes

Tidewater Amelia is a great photographic work, of homes and buildings, detailing the history of Nassau County, Florida, and surrounding communities. Lexington Ventures/ISBN 0-9677419-2-0

Yesterday's Reflections II
Jan H. Johannes

This book is more than a picturesque chronology of events detailing our place in the passage of time. It is a passport that takes the reader on a journey through time in Nassau County, Florida, and surrounding areas. Lexington Ventures/ ISBN 0-9677419-0-4

Images of America: Cumberland Island
Patricia Barefoot

Great images of local heritage. Founded in 1893, the African Baptist Church cornerstone carries the names of Ms. Beulah G. Alberty, church clerk, and Rev. L. Morrison, pastor, both of whom served at New Zion Baptist Church. Also see restored home and brief history about Ms. Alberty, page 28. Arcadia Publishing/ISBN 978-0-7385-1650-9

The Golden Age of Amelia Island (Revised)
Suzanne Davis Hardee / Kathleen Davis Hardee Arsenault

A comprehensive history of Amelia Island from the end of the Civil War to the end of the 1910s. Lexington Ventures/ ISBN 978-1934401057

"If you want to understand today,
you have to search yesterday."

~ Pearl Buck

ABOUT THE AUTHOR

Annette Myers is a National Indie Excellence Award winning author. She is a Fernandina Beach, Florida, native, community activist, and a retired Nassau County educator. She has taught in the public school system of Florida on various levels, including Florida State College of Jacksonville. Since retirement, she has published three non-fiction books about historic American Beach. American Beach lies on the south end of Amelia Island in Fernandina Beach.

Annette is well-traveled in and out of the United States. Her home is American Beach, in northeast Florida, where she is a longtime property owner and the owner of Martha's Hideaway. Her home, Martha's Hideaway, was listed on the National Register of Historic Places October 12, 2001.

Annette earned her Bachelor of Science degree from Florida A. & M. University in Tallahassee, Florida, Master of Science degree from Indiana State University, Terre Haute, Indiana, and her Educational Specialist degree from Nova University in Fort Lauderdale, Florida.

She is the proud mother of son Donald Myers (wife Dedria), grandchild Delaney Ann Myers and foster daughter Alria Wilson Mundy.

OTHER NON-FICTION BOOKS BY ANNETTE MYERS

The Shrinking Sands of an African American Beach
– 1ˢᵗ Edition

The Shrinking Sands of an African American Beach
– Revised Edition

The Big Sand Dune and The Beach Lady

www.ingramcontent.com/pod-product-compliance
Lightning Source LLC
Chambersburg PA
CBHW041711260326
41914CB00038B/1991/J